A LOOK AT PRIMARY SOURCES

ARTWORK

BY KRISTEN RAJCZAK NELSON

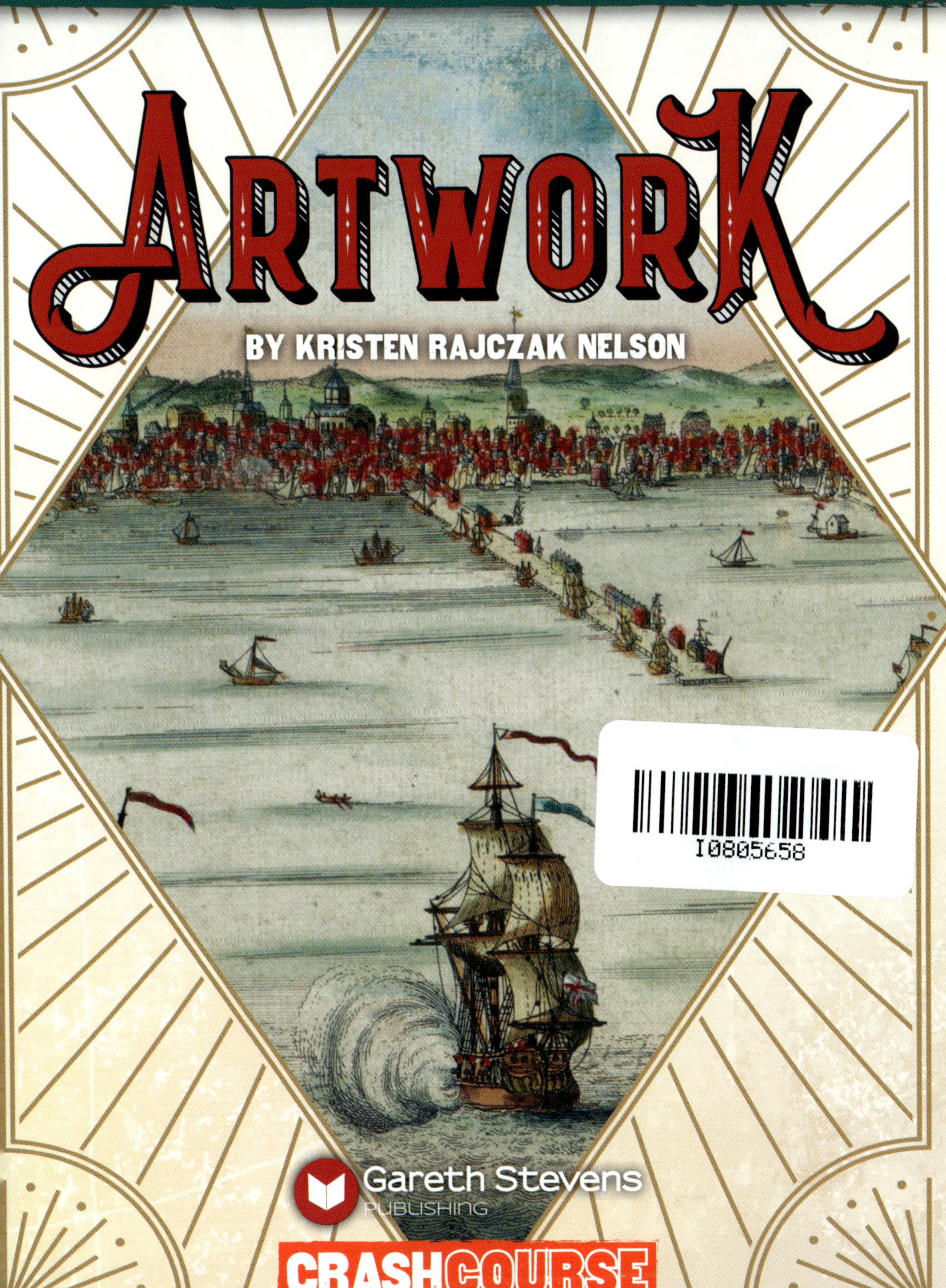

Gareth Stevens PUBLISHING

CRASHCOURSE

Please visit our website, www.garethstevens.com. For a free color catalog of all our high-quality books, call toll free 1-800-542-2595 or fax 1-877-542-2596.

Library of Congress Cataloging-in-Publication Data
Names: Rajczak Nelson, Kristen, author.
Title: Artwork / Kristen Rajczak Nelson.
Description: Buffalo, New York : Gareth Stevens Publishing, [2024] |
Series: A look at primary sources | Includes index.
Identifiers: LCCN 2022054818 (print) | LCCN 2022054819 (ebook) | ISBN 9781538287446 (library binding) | ISBN 9781538287439 (paperback) | ISBN 9781538287453 (ebook)
Subjects: LCSH: Art appreciation--Juvenile literature.
Classification: LCC N7477 .R35 2024 (print) | LCC N7477 (ebook) | DDC 701/.18--dc23/eng/20221229
LC record available at https://lccn.loc.gov/2022054818
LC ebook record available at https://lccn.loc.gov/2022054819

First Edition

Published in 2024 by
Gareth Stevens Publishing
2544 Clinton Street
Buffalo, NY 14224

Designer: Claire Wrazin
Editor: Kristen Rajczak Nelson

Photo credits: Cover (art) courtesy of the Library of Congress; series art (background texture) Verbena/Shutterstock.com; series art (cover typeface) Gleb Guralnyk/Shutterstock.com; p. 5 Anton_Ivanov/Shutterstock.com; p. 7 (artwork) File:The_Death_of_General_Warren_at_the_Battle_of_Bunker's_Hill.jpg/Wikimedia Commons; p. 7 (bottom) Valeriy Karpeev/Shutterstock.com; pp. 7, 17, 21 (gold frames) TR STOK/Shutterstock.com; pp. 7, 25 (photo frame) Nataliia K/Shutterstock.com; p. 9 (artwork) File:Johannes_Vermeer_(1632-1675)_-_The_Girl_With_The_Pearl_Earring_(1665).jpg/Wikimedia Commons; p. 9 (background) Followtheflow/Shutterstock.com; p. 11 File:Boston_Tea_Party_w.jpg/Wikimedia Commons; p. 13 (artwork) File:Declaration_of_Independence_(1819),_by_John_Trumbull.jpg/Wikimedia Commons; p. 13 (frame) Andrej Antic/Shutterstock.com; p. 15 (artwork) File:1_of_May,_1851.jpg/Wikimedia Commons; p. 15 (background) Hunter Bliss Images/Shutterstock.com; p. 17 (artwork) File:The Fighting Temeraire, JMW Turner, National Gallery.jpg/Wikimedai Commons; p. 19 (artwork) File:Juan_Gris_-_Portrait_of_Pablo_Picasso_-_Google_Art _Project.jpg/Wikimedia Commons; p. 19 (background) Kutlayev Dmitry/Shutterstock.com; p. 21 (artwork) File:Juan_Gris_-_Violine_und_Glas_-_1913.jpeg/Wikimedia Commons; p. 23 File:Vincent_van_Gogh_- _Self-Portrait_-_Google_Art_Project_(454045).jpg/Wikimedia Commons; p. 25 (top) File:Auguste_Rodin_-_Head_of_Balzac.jpg/Wikimedia Commons; p. 25 (right) File:Auguste_Rodin_Pensee_Gsell_203.jpg/Wikimedia Commons; p. 25 (bottom) File:The_Thinker_MET_131262.jpg/Wikimedia Commons; p. 25 (arrows) Lyudmyla Ishchenko/Shutterstock.com; p. 27 Pressmaster/Shutterstock.com; p. 29 SeventyFour/Shutterstock.com

Printed in the United States of America

CPSIA compliance information: Batch #CS24GS: For further information contact Gareth Stevens at 1-800-542-2595.

CONTENTS

Words in the glossary appear in **bold** type the first time they are used in the text.

WHAT IS ART?

Artwork includes paintings, drawings, and **sculptures**. Art may be presented for its beauty. It can make a statement about the world around us. By looking at art, we can learn. That's because art is often a primary source!

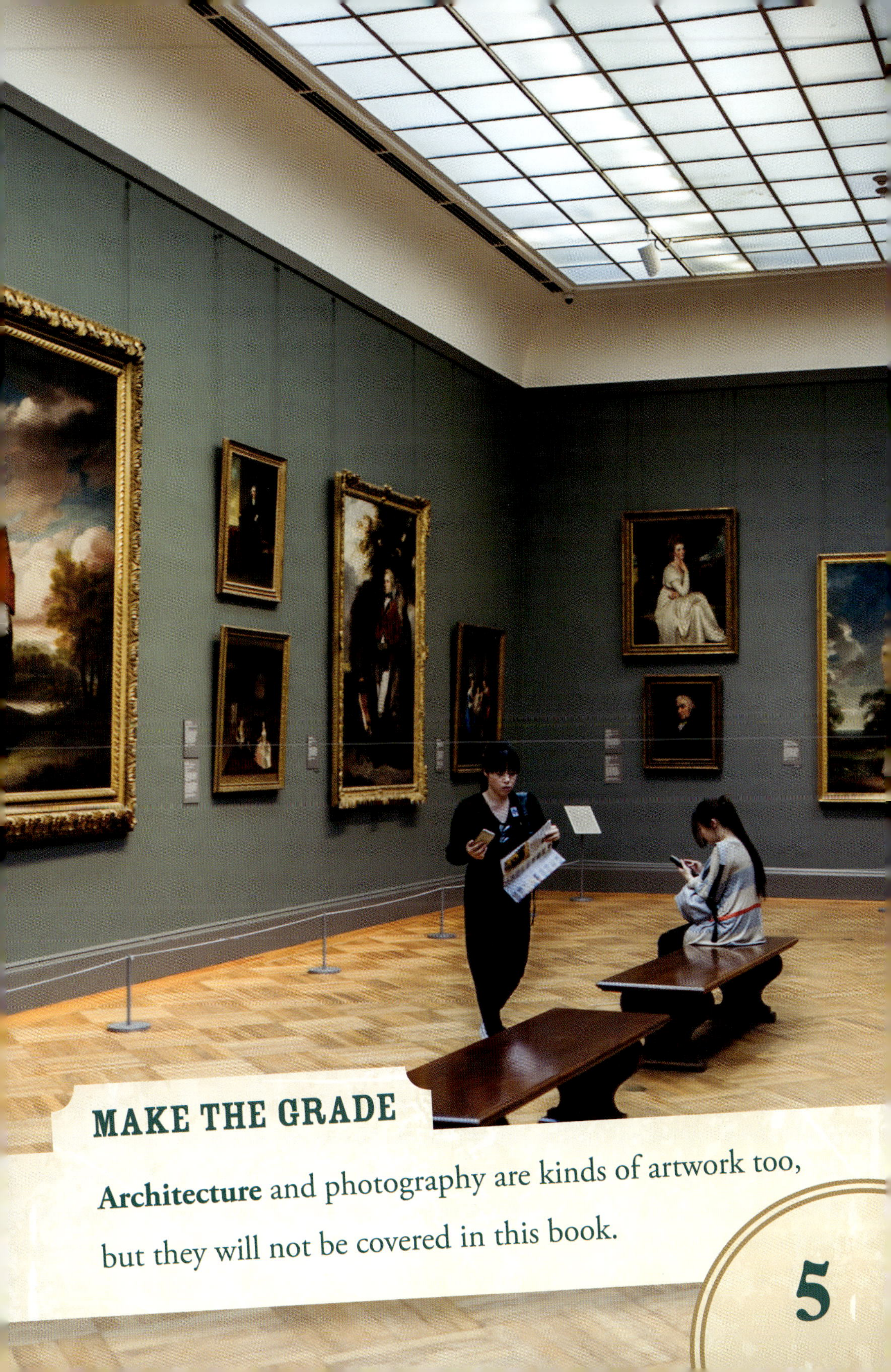

MAKE THE GRADE

Architecture and photography are kinds of artwork too, but they will not be covered in this book.

THE FIRST SOURCE

"Primary" means first. A primary source is something that contains firsthand **information**. It was made by someone directly connected, or tied, to what the source is about. They may have lived during a certain time. They may have been present when something important happened.

MAKE THE GRADE

A secondary source is something created using primary sources, such as a history book. It often **interprets** the primary source.

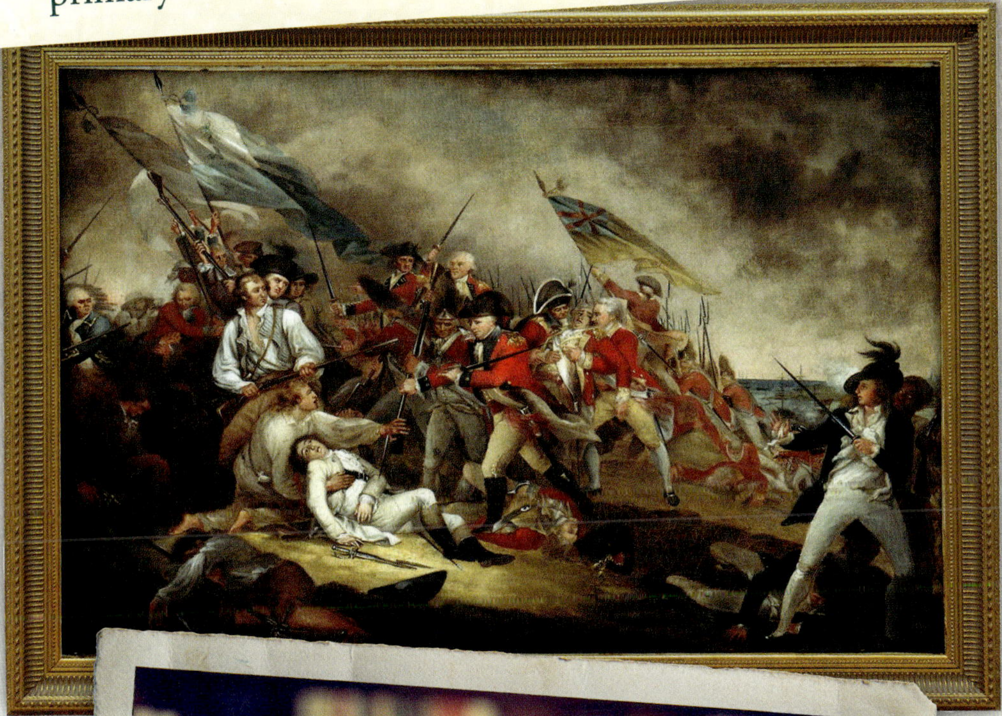

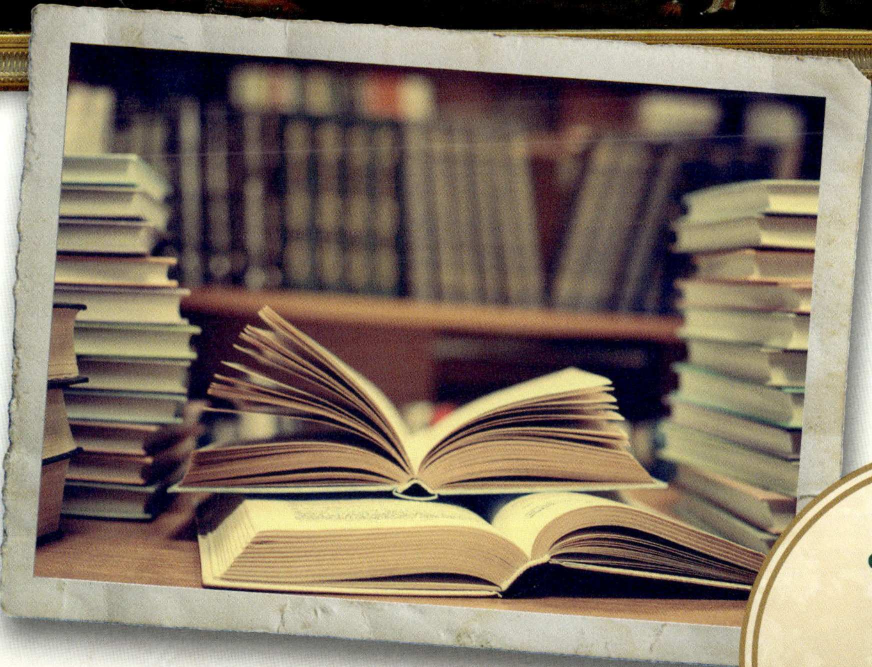

Most famous art is kept in **museums**. You might only see a picture in a book. You don't have to see artwork in person to use it as a primary source though. Even **reproductions** of artwork may be used as a primary source.

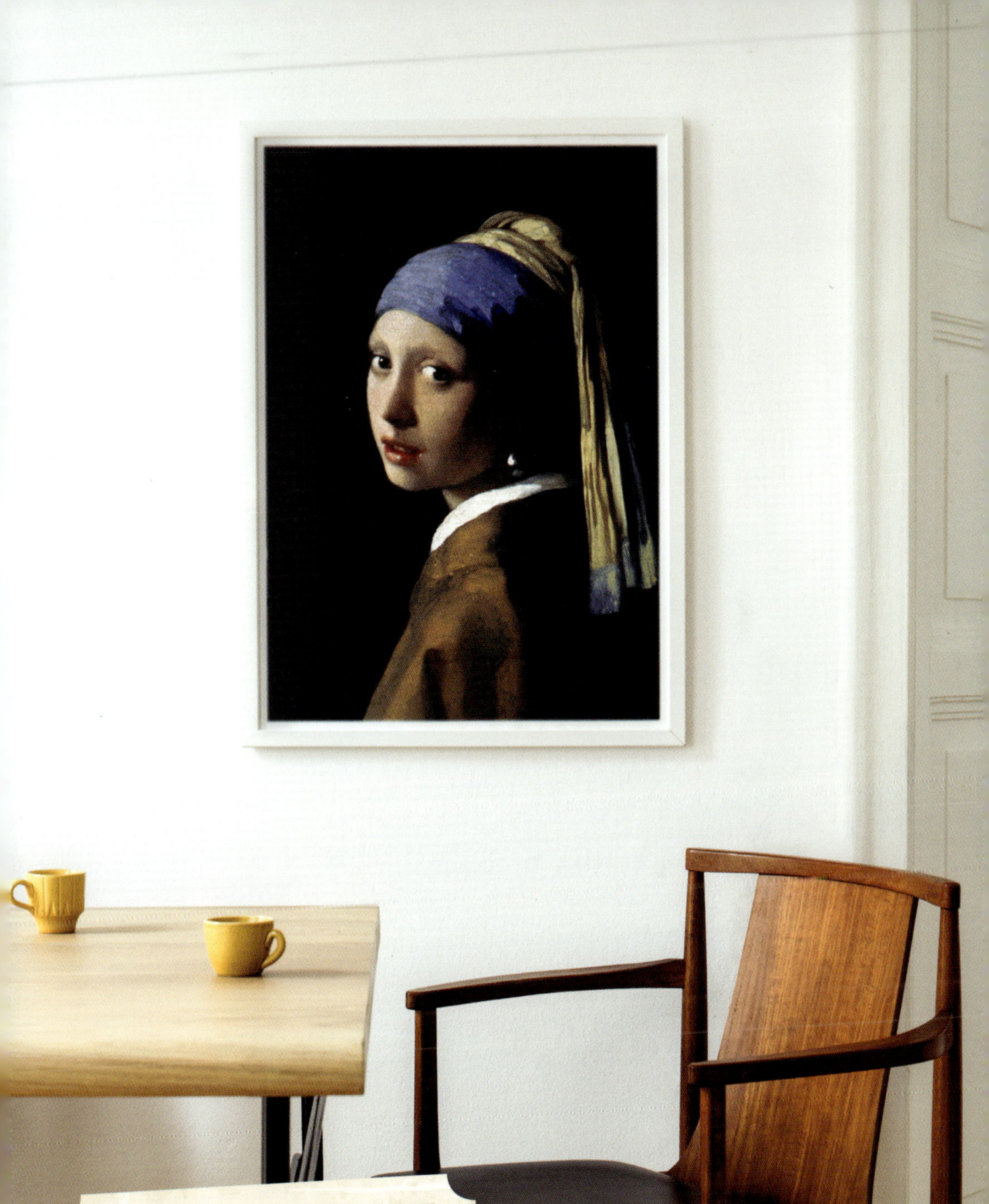

MAKE THE GRADE

Sometimes reproductions aren't exactly the same as a piece of art. The colors may be just a little different. It will likely be a different size.

HOW TO USE IT

Art can be used as a primary source in a few ways. Before photography, art, such as drawings, **engravings**, and paintings, showed what happened at events. Today, historians look at the art to understand historical events better.

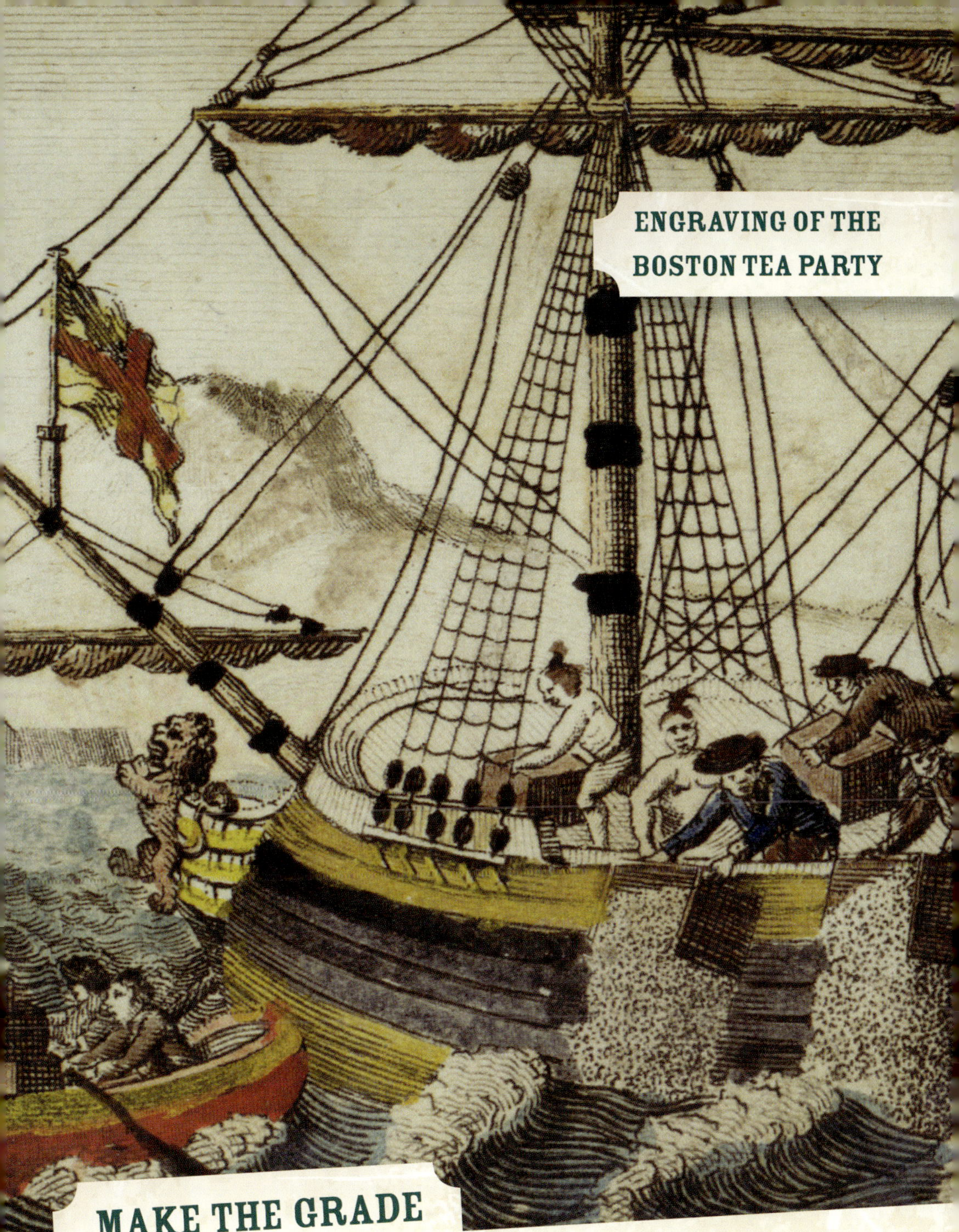

ENGRAVING OF THE BOSTON TEA PARTY

MAKE THE GRADE

Art is created from the **perspective** of the artist. Because of this, historians use artwork as just one source to inform what happened in history.

HISTORIC ART

Painter John Trumbull was **commissioned** to create a work that showed the signing of the Declaration of Independence. Trumbull painted many of the Founding Fathers from life. It is one artwork that shows how they really looked! We might not know otherwise.

MAKE THE GRADE

Trumbull's *Declaration of Independence* hangs in the U.S. Capitol.

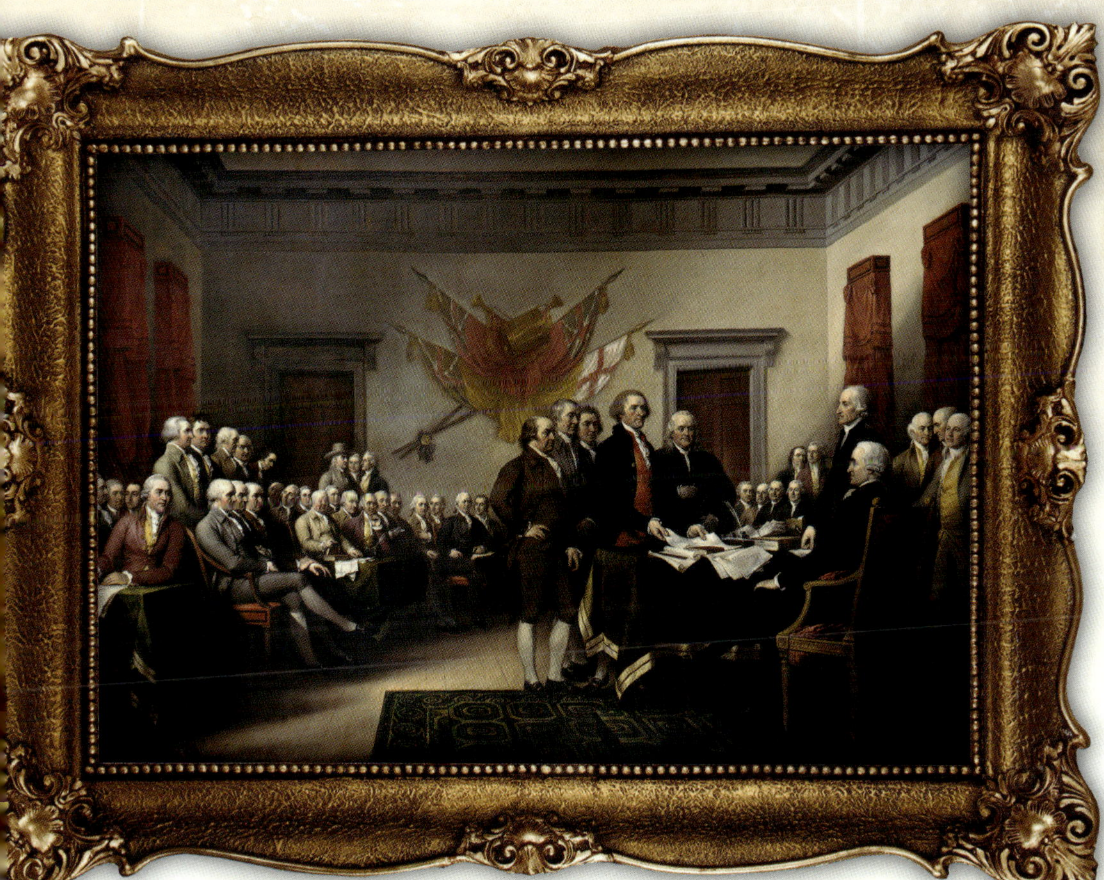

JOHN TRUMBULL
DECLARATION OF INDEPENDENCE
1818

OF THE TIME

Art displayed in a museum or online will have a title. It will list the date it was finished. This information tells what time period the artwork can be used as a primary source for.

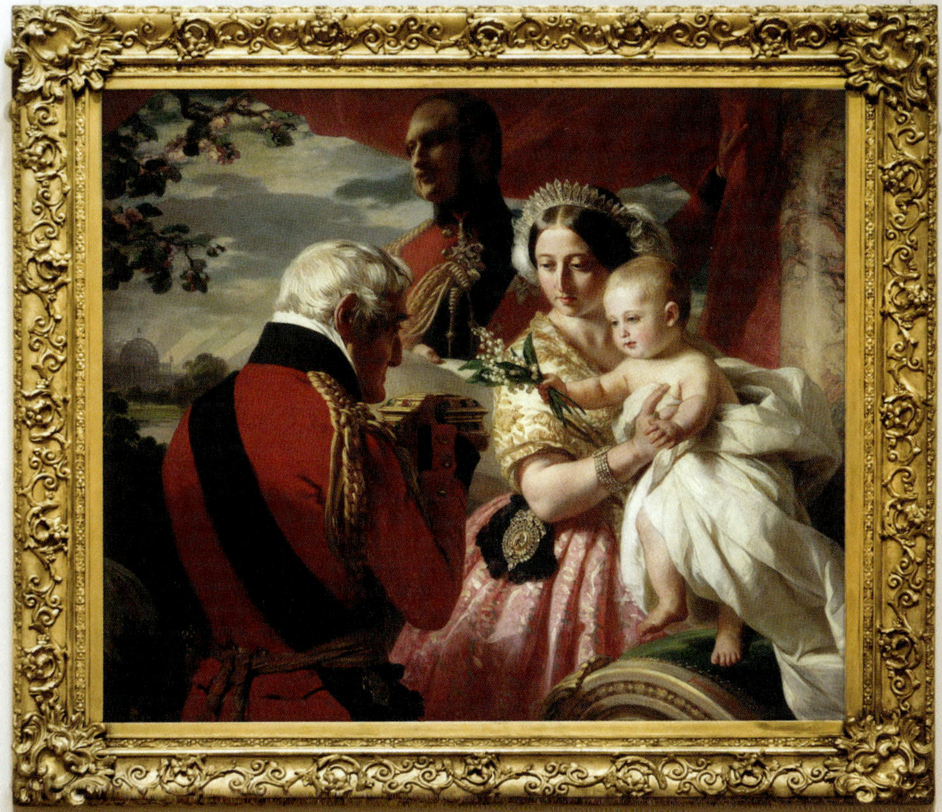

MAKE THE GRADE

Even without a title or date, you can often use the clues in a piece of art, such as what people are wearing, to figure out when it's from.

The scene shown in a piece of art may also show about the time it was created. In *The Fighting Temeraire*, artist J. M. W. Turner shows the last sail of a great warship. It showed the changes of the **Industrial Revolution**.

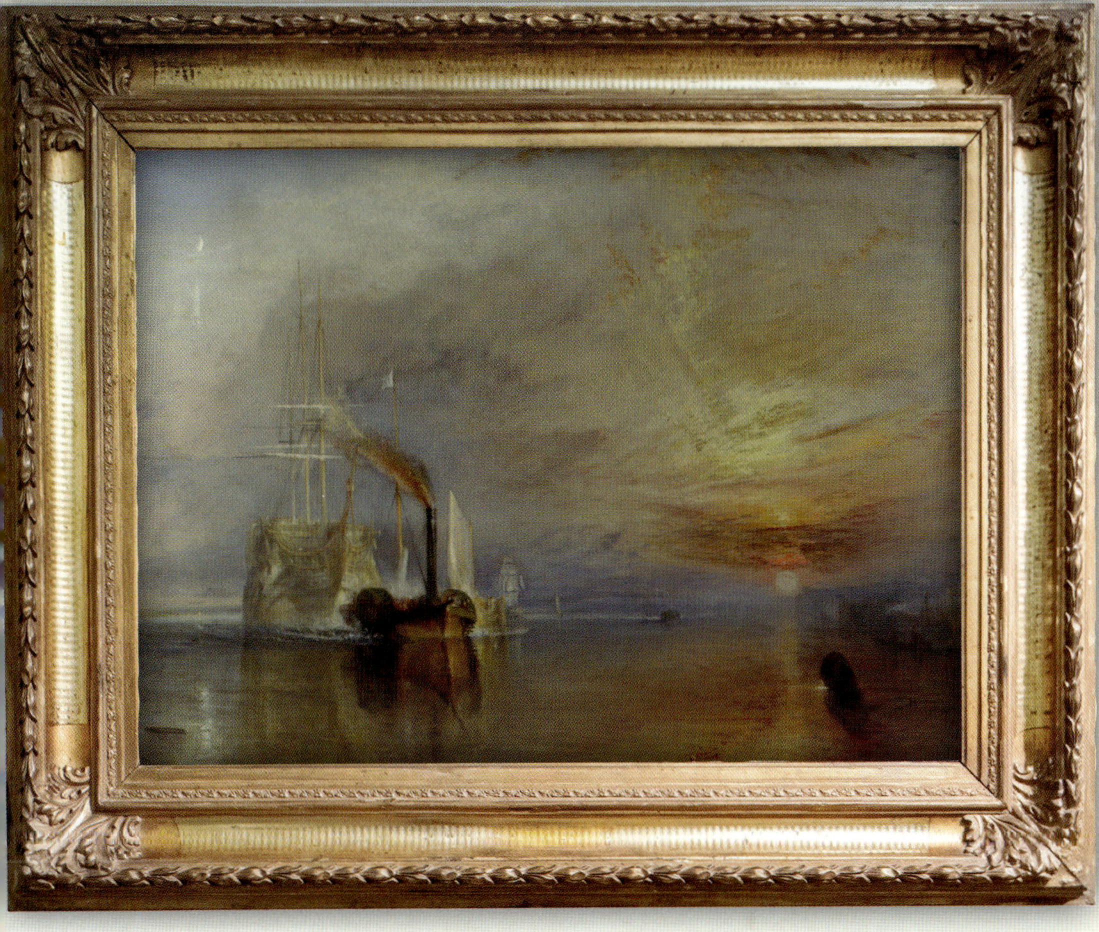

J. M. W. TURNER
THE FIGHTING TEMERAIRE
1839

MAKE THE GRADE

The Fighting Temeraire hangs in the National Gallery in London, England.

MANY MOVEMENTS

Art can teach about the art movement during which it was made. An art movement is a period of time when many artists followed a certain style. It can also be when artists followed a certain **philosophy** or had a goal in their art.

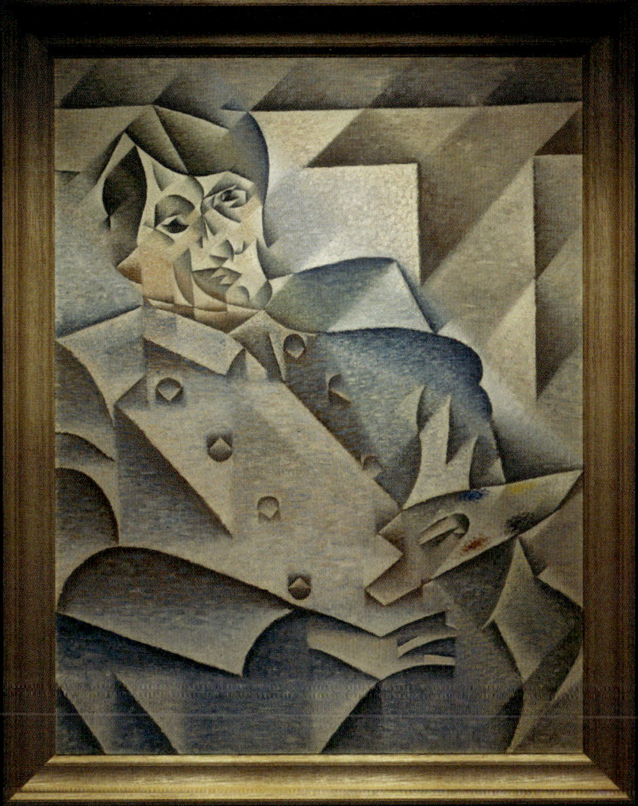

JUAN GRIS
PORTRAIT OF PABLO PICASSO
1912

MAKE THE GRADE

Movements in art can last a few months, a few years, or longer!

Cubism is one artistic movement that began in the early 1900s. It showed many ways to see something all in one piece of art. It looked fragmented, or broken apart. Spanish painter Juan Gris's work is part of the Cubist movement.

MAKE THE GRADE

Pablo Picasso and Georges Braque are commonly credited as the artists that started Cubism.

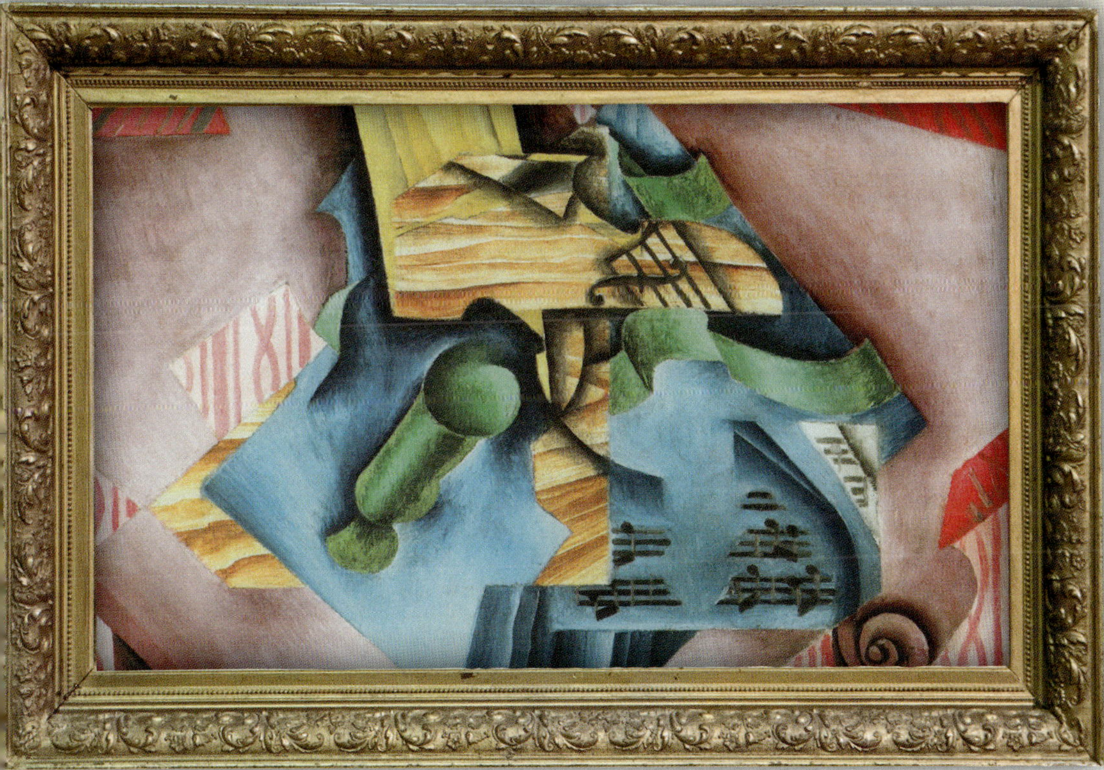

JUAN GRIS
VIOLIN AND GLASS
1913

AN ARTISTIC LIFE

A piece of art can serve as a primary source when learning about an artist. Vincent Van Gogh, for example, painted many self-portraits. They show what he looked like through his own eyes. They also show how he was feeling.

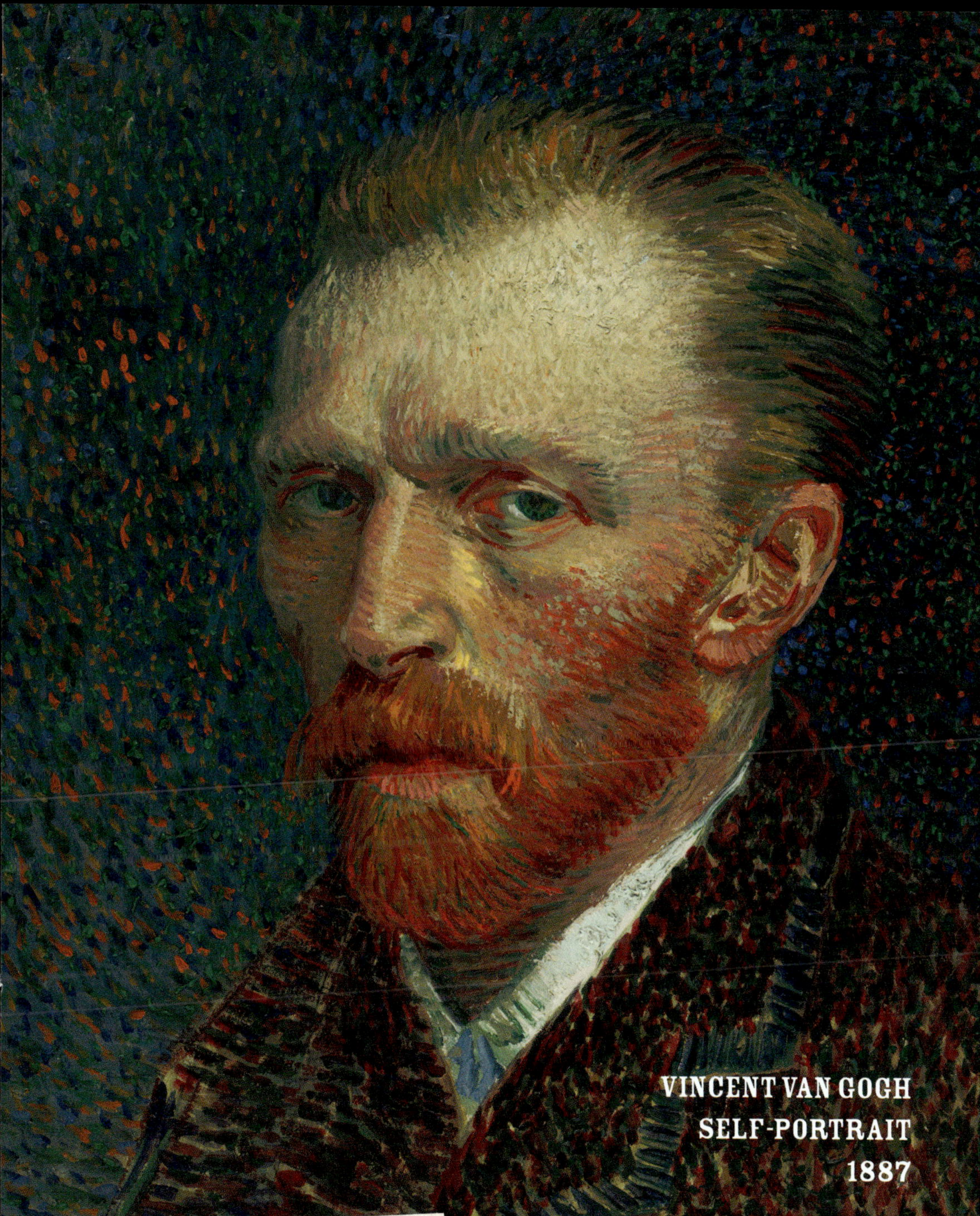

VINCENT VAN GOGH
SELF-PORTRAIT
1887

MAKE THE GRADE

A self-portrait is a drawing or painting done of an artist, by the artist.

Looking at many pieces of art by one artist can show how their work has changed over time. They can show what an artist was interested in. Auguste Rodin sculpted many portraits, including *The Thinker.*

MAKE THE GRADE

Rodin sculpted his works out of marble and bronze.

Head of Balzac
modeled 1897,
cast early 1900s

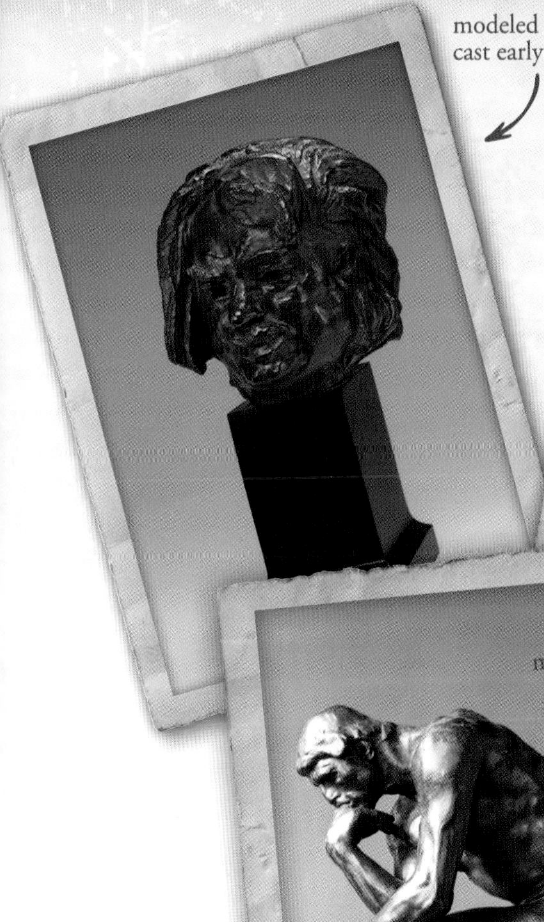

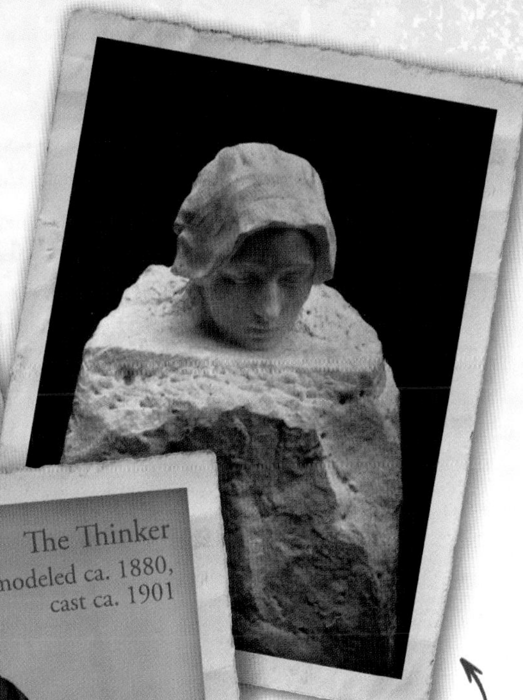

Thought
modeled 1895,
cast 1901

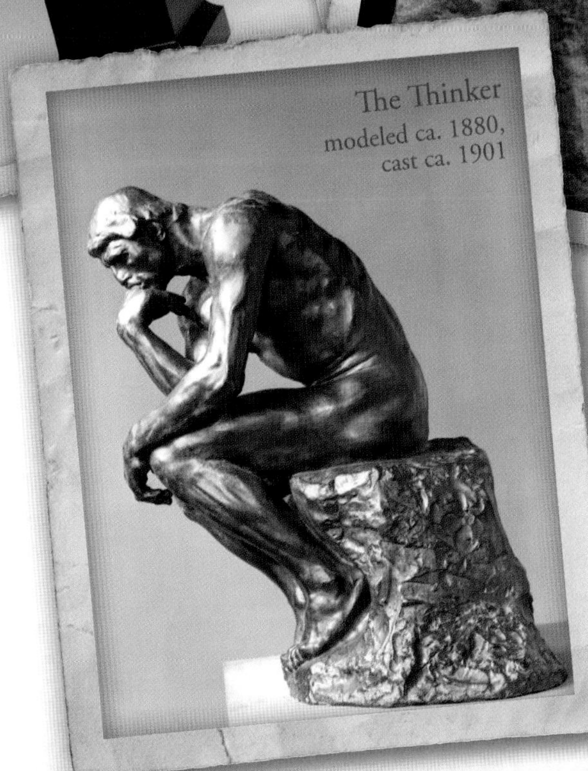

The Thinker
modeled ca. 1880,
cast ca. 1901

OTHER PRIMARY SOURCES

To learn about an artist, looking at other primary sources beyond artwork is helpful. Some artists wrote letters that tell about how they made art. They may be about their daily life! Artists may write an autobiography, or book, about their life.

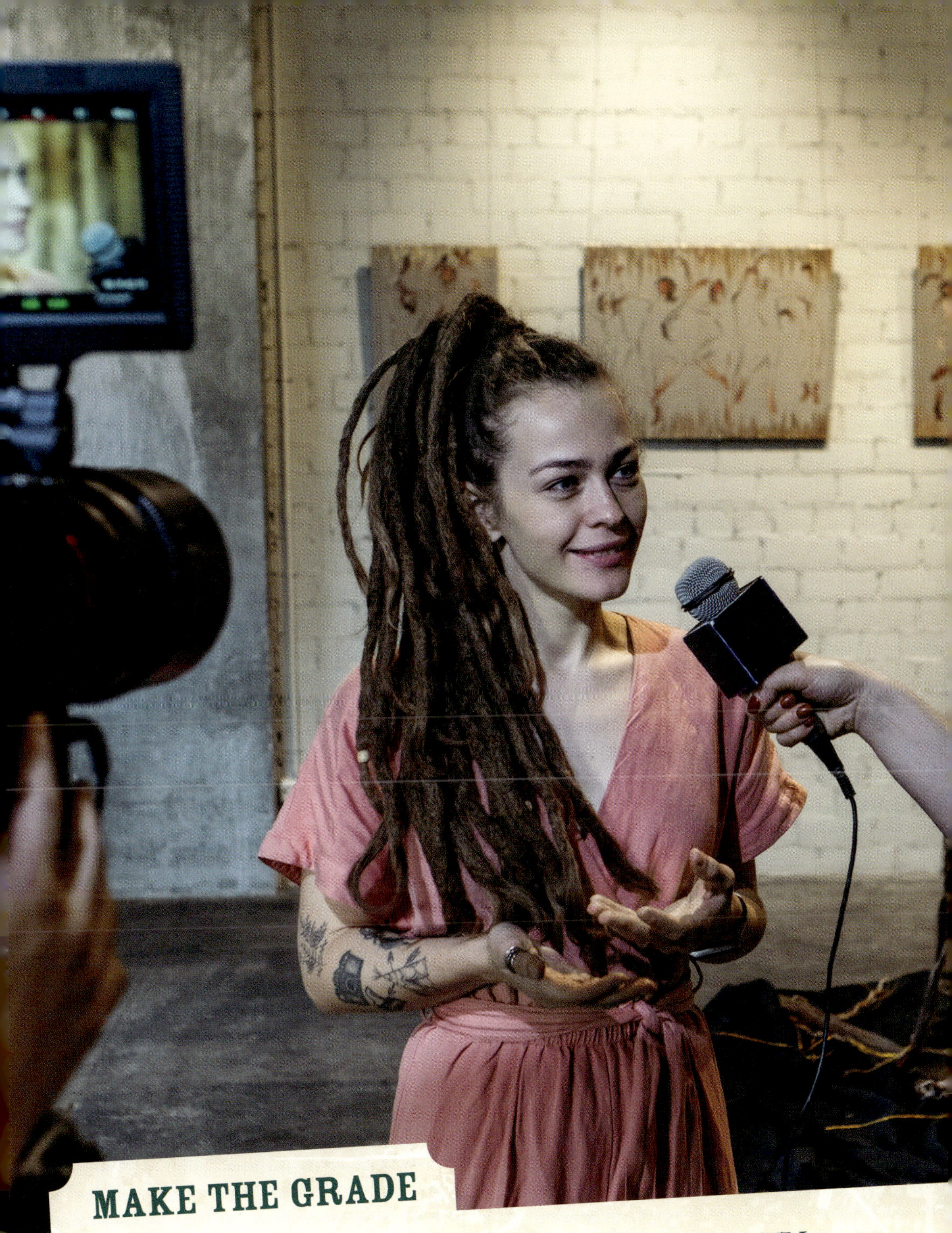

MAKE THE GRADE

Today's artists may even talk about their work on TV or online! These are primary sources too.

DIGITAL ART

It's never been easier to use art as a primary source! Many museums have online collections. You can often see the art closer than if you saw it in person. This allows you to think even more about what it can teach you.

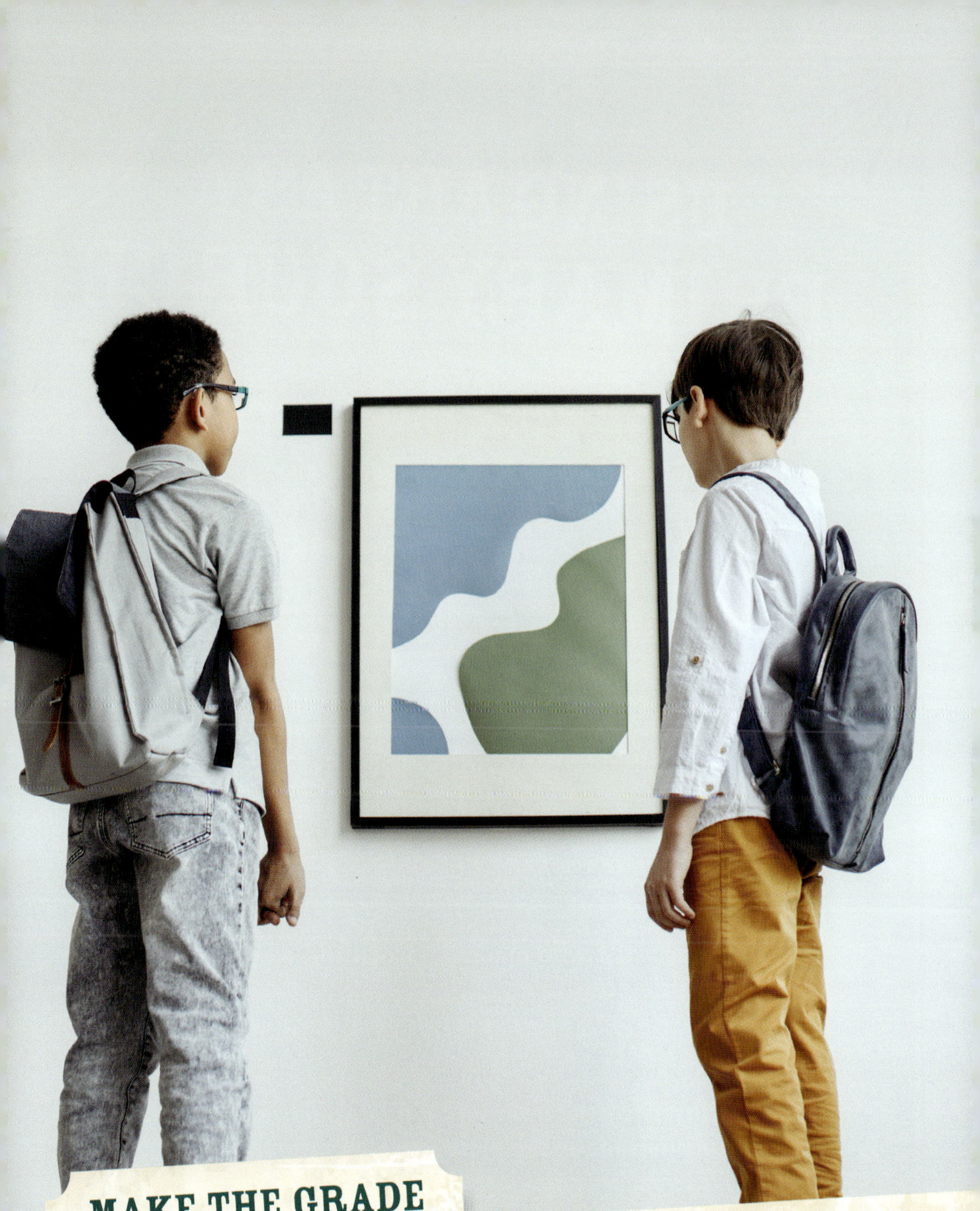

MAKE THE GRADE

You don't have to visit a well-known museum to see art. Many cities have art museums you can visit today!

USING ART AS A PRIMARY SOURCE

Visit the online collections of one of the following museums:
The National Gallery of Art, Washington, D.C.
Musée d'Orsay, Paris, France
Van Gogh Museum, Amsterdam, Netherlands
The British Museum, London, England

Choose a piece of artwork.
- *Why did you pick it?*

Record your first thoughts about the art. Do this without looking at any additional information about the piece. Answer these questions:
- *What does the artwork show?*
- *How does it make you feel?*
- *What does it make you think about?*

Find out the artist who made the work and when they made it. Find out the title.
- *What clues does this information give you about how this piece of art could be used as a primary source?*

Use the library or the internet to look up more about the artist, time period, or the piece itself.
- *How did secondary sources change your thoughts about the artwork?*
- *When would this piece of art be a secondary source instead of a primary source?*

GLOSSARY

architecture: The art of designing buildings.

commission: To be hired to make a piece of art.

engraving: The art of cutting a picture into the surface of material like wood or metal. Also, a picture made from an engraved surface.

Industrial Revolution: An era of social and economic change marked by advances in technology and science.

information: Knowledge obtained from study or observation.

interpret: To explain the meaning of something.

museum: A place in which art, valuable items, or objects from history are kept and shown to the public.

perspective: The way of thinking about and understanding something.

philosophy: A system of thought made to try to understand the nature of that which is real.

reproduction: A copy.

sculpture: A kind of artwork made by carving or molding stone, clay, metal, or other material.

FOR MORE INFORMATION

BOOKS

Boswell, Kelly. *Research Visual Primary Sources: Photographs, Painting, Video, and More!* Mankato, MN: Pebble, an imprint of Capstone, 2019.

Halls, Kelly Milner. *Famous Artists in History: 15 Painters, Sculptors, and Photographers You Should Know.* Oakland, CA: Rockridge Press, 2022.

WEBSITE

MetKids

www.metmuseum.org/art/online-features/metkids/

Explore the artwork of one the most famous museums in the world!

Publisher's note to educators and parents: Our editors have carefully reviewed these websites to ensure that they are suitable for students. Many websites change frequently, however, and we cannot guarantee that a site's future contents will continue to meet our high standards of quality and educational value. Be advised that students should be closely supervised whenever they access the internet.

INDEX